Rainbow Loom®

Jewelry Made Easy!

Here is everything you need to know to start making bracelets, rings, & more fun stuff with your Rainbow Loom®. Simple diagrams & instructions explain every step. You'll have a blast making these projects & impressing your friends!

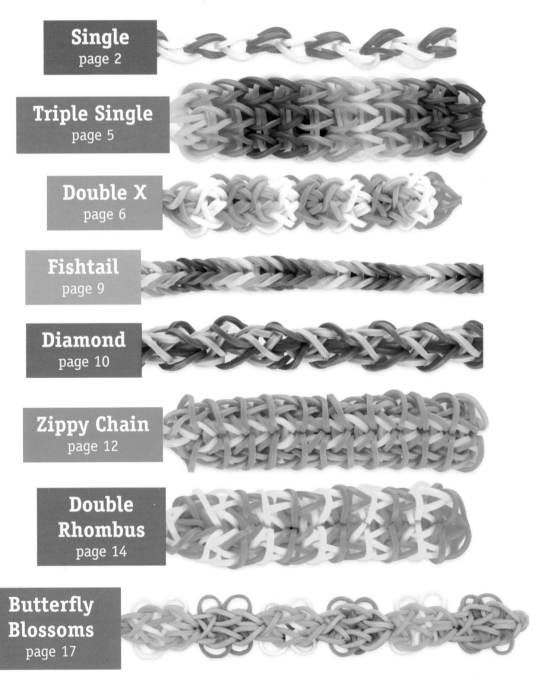

Single
page 2

Triple Single
page 5

Double X
page 6

Fishtail
page 9

Diamond
page 10

Zippy Chain
page 12

Double Rhombus
page 14

Butterfly Blossoms
page 17

LEISURE ARTS, INC. • Little Rock, Arkansas

The Rainbow Loom®

The Rainbow Loom is a series of plastic pins joined together in rows. Bracelets, necklaces, & rings are made by placing elastic bands on the loom pins & looping them over each other in a pattern. Each project will have a Diagram to place the bands, as well as illustrations to show looping the bands.

To the right is a picture of the loom & a blank Diagram that will show band placement. Each ∪ shape represents a loom pin.

The band's color & direction are shown on the Diagram & illustrations. It's very important to follow the Steps when placing & looping the bands on the loom pins.

On the illustrations, the band that you are working with is shown in color. Bands that are in the background or not being used for that Step are shown in a much lighter color.

Let's get started with a basic Single Bracelet in red & white where you'll learn to place & loop the bands.

Loom

Diagram

Pin

Pin

Single

Photos on page 4.

Band Placement

Place the loom on the table with the loom arrows pointing away from you. This bracelet only uses 2 rows of pins.

Step 1: Use your fingers to place a red band on the loom. Push it down on the pins.

Step 2: Then add a white band & push it down on the pins.

Step 3: Continue to place red & white bands on the loom pins until you reach the top of the loom (see the Diagram on page 3).

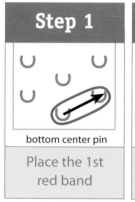

Step 1

bottom center pin

Place the 1st red band

Step 2

Place the 1st white band

Looping

When Looping the Bands:

- Turn the loom around so the arrows are pointing toward you.
- Always use the looping tool to pick up & loop the bands.

Step 1: Use the looping tool to go down into the center pin hole. Move the red band out of the way & grab the white band with the hook. Pull it up & off the pin.

Step 2: Keeping the band on the hook, loop the white band over the pin to the left; remove the hook.

Step 3: Go down into the next pin hole on the left & pick up the red band. Pull it up & off the pin.

Step 4: Loop the red band over to the center pin.

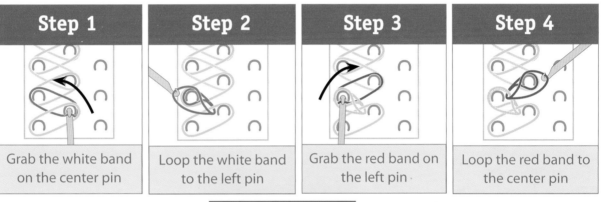

Step 1	Step 2	Step 3	Step 4
Grab the white band on the center pin	Loop the white band to the left pin	Grab the red band on the left pin	Loop the red band to the center pin

Step 5: Continue picking up & looping the red & white bands until you've looped the last red band.

Step 6: Slide a C-clip over the red band loops.

Step 6

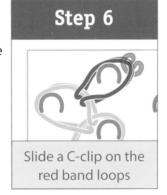

Slide a C-clip on the red band loops

Step 7: Carefully pull all the bands from the pins.

Step 8: Join the bracelet by slipping the C-clip through the loop at the beginning of the bracelet.

Congratulations! You've just made your first Rainbow Loom Bracelet! Make several of these in different colors to practice working with the looping tool. You can also make a ring to match your bracelet using 9-10 bands.

Triple Single
(page 5)

Single
(pages 2-3)

riple Single

Photos on page 4.

Band Placement

The illustrations show the rainbow version of the bracelet.

The stripes are formed by straight lines of elastic bands; the base under the stripes is formed by bands that are placed on the pins in triangles.

When Placing the Bands:

- Place the loom on the table with the arrows pointing away from you.
- Use your fingers to place the bands on the loom.
- Follow the Steps when placing the bands.
- Push each band down after you place it on the pins.

teps 1-3:
ace bands on
ch pin row,
arting with yellow
referring to the
oto (above) for
lor sequence.

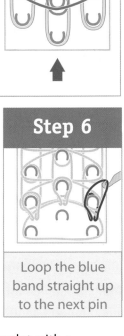

Diagram

Step 1	Step 2	Step 3
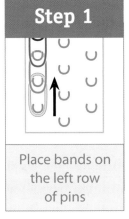	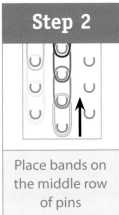	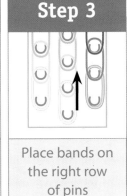
Place bands on the left row of pins	Place bands on the middle row of pins	Place bands on the right row of pins

Step 4:
Place white bands in triangles as shown on the Diagram.

Looping

When Looping the Bands:

- Turn the loom around so the arrows are pointing toward you.
- Always use the looping tool to pick up & loop the bands.

Step 1	Step 2	Step 3	Step 4	Step 5	Step 6
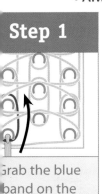	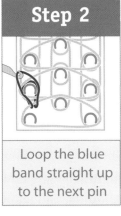	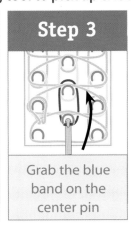	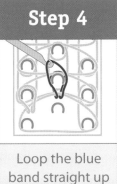	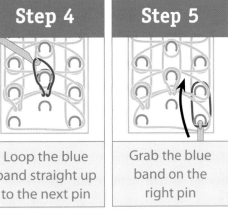	
rab the blue band on the left pin	Loop the blue band straight up to the next pin	Grab the blue band on the center pin	Loop the blue band straight up to the next pin	Grab the blue band on the right pin	Loop the blue band straight up to the next pin

ep 7: Continue picking up & looping the bands until you reach the top of the loom. Finish the bracelet with a hite extension & C-clip (see pages 19-20).

Tips: Our color combos (see page 4) include red, white, & blue stripes with a white base & extension, blue, green, & aqua stripes with a black base & extension, & aqua, green, & purple stripes with a yellow base & extension. The bracelet without an extension looks great on a spring-closure barrette; just tie the end loops to the barrette ends.

Double X

Photos on pages 7 & 8.

Band Placement

The illustrations show the pink, white, & green version of the bracelet.
This bracelet requires you to rearrange the pin rows so the pins line up horizontally. Elastic bands are placed on the loom pins in a Double X pattern.

Use the large hook to loosen the blue bases on the loom.

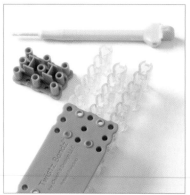

Remove the bases.

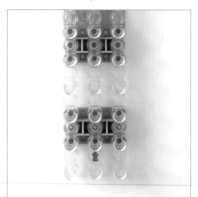

Line up the pin rows so they are even on the ends & replace the bases.

When Placing the Bands:

- Place the loom on the table with the arrows pointing away from you.
- Use your fingers to place the bands on the loom.
- Follow the Steps when placing the bands.
- Push each band down after you place it on the pins.

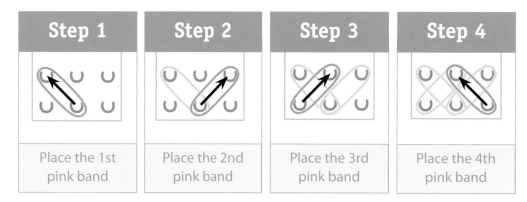

Step 1	Step 2	Step 3	Step 4
Place the 1st pink band	Place the 2nd pink band	Place the 3rd pink band	Place the 4th pink band

Step 5: Moving up the loom, repeat with 4 white bands & then 4 green bands. Continue to place the pink, white, & green bands on the loom pins until you reach the top of the loom (see the Diagram above).

Double X
(pages 6-8)

Fishtail
(page 9)

Looping

When Looping the Bands:

- Turn the loom around so the arrows are pointing toward you.
- Always use the looping tool to pick up & loop the bands.

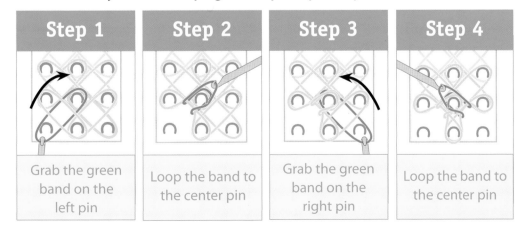

Step 1	Step 2	Step 3	Step 4
Grab the green band on the left pin	Loop the band to the center pin	Grab the green band on the right pin	Loop the band to the center pin

Double X continued on page 8.

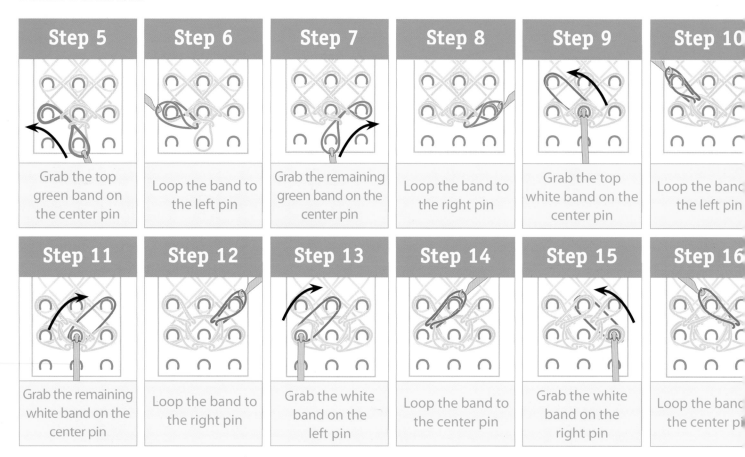

Step 5	Step 6	Step 7	Step 8	Step 9	Step 10
Grab the top green band on the center pin	Loop the band to the left pin	Grab the remaining green band on the center pin	Loop the band to the right pin	Grab the top white band on the center pin	Loop the band the left pin

Step 11	Step 12	Step 13	Step 14	Step 15	Step 16
Grab the remaining white band on the center pin	Loop the band to the right pin	Grab the white band on the left pin	Loop the band to the center pin	Grab the white band on the right pin	Loop the band the center pi

Step 17: Repeating from Step 9, continue to pick up & loop the pink, green, & white bands until you've looped the last set of bands.

Step 18: Finish the bracelet with a pink, white, & green extension & a C-clip (see pages 19-20).

Tips: The photos on page 7 & below show several other color combinations, substituting blue, red, & yellow for the pink, white, & green; using a completely different color for each set of X's; or arranging a repeating rainbow of colors. You can tie the loops at the beginning & end of the bracelet (don't make an extension) to a spring-closure barrette too.

Fishtail

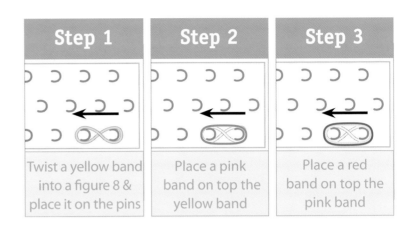

Photos on page 7 & 8.

Band Placement

…e illustrations show the rainbow version of the bracelet. …is four-sided bracelet is made on just 2 side-by-side …om pins.

When Placing the Bands:

…urn the loom so the arrows are pointing to the left.
…Use your fingers to place the bands on the loom.
…ollow the Steps when placing the bands.
…ush each band down after you place it on the pins.

Step 1	**Step 2**	**Step 3**
Twist a yellow band into a figure 8 & place it on the pins	Place a pink band on top the yellow band	Place a red band on top the pink band

Looping

When Looping the Bands:

• Always use the looping tool to pick up & loop the bands.

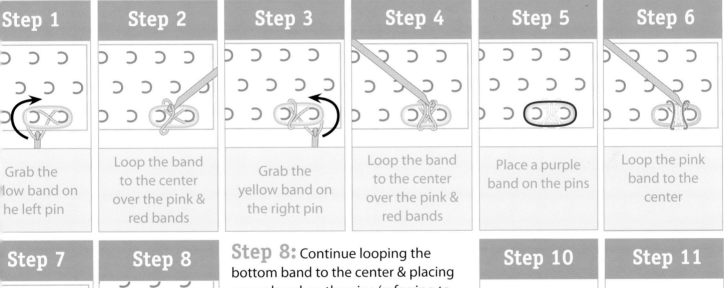

Step 1	**Step 2**	**Step 3**	**Step 4**	**Step 5**	**Step 6**
Grab the …low band on …he left pin	Loop the band to the center over the pink & red bands	Grab the yellow band on the right pin	Loop the band to the center over the pink & red bands	Place a purple band on the pins	Loop the pink band to the center

Step 7	**Step 8**
…lace a blue …and on the pins	Continue looping the bottom band to the center

Step 8: Continue looping the bottom band to the center & placing a new band on the pins (referring to the photo above for color sequence). The bracelet will extend between the 2 pins.

Step 9: When the bracelet is long enough, loop the bottom band to center.

Step 10	**Step 11**

Grab the last band from the pins & slide it on the hook	Slide a C-clip on the band loops at the beginning & end to join

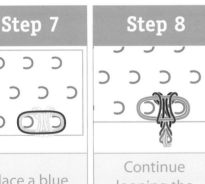

Tips: Other color combinations (shown in the photos on pages 7 & 8) are easy—for two colors, alternate the colors on the pins; for three colors, just repeat the color sequence.

Diamond

Photos on pages 11 & 12.

Band Placement

The illustrations show the blue & aqua version of the bracelet.
This bracelet looks great with 2 colors or in a rainbow of hues.

When Placing the Bands:

- Place the loom on the table with the arrows pointing away from you.
- Use your fingers to place the bands on the loom.
- Follow the Steps when placing the bands.
- Push each band down after you place it on the pins.

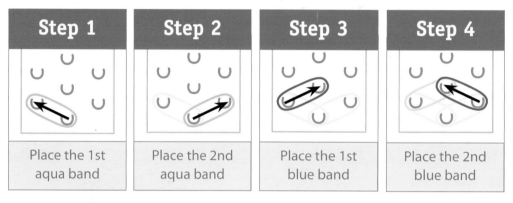

Step 1	Step 2	Step 3	Step 4
Place the 1st aqua band	Place the 2nd aqua band	Place the 1st blue band	Place the 2nd blue band

Step 5: Ending with 1 aqua band at the top, continue to place the aqua & blue bands on the loom pins until you reach the top of the loom (see the Diagram to the right).

> **Color Tips:** Team colors make fun bracelets; try purple & yellow, red & black, purple & green, pink & white, or even rainbow hues.

Looping

When Looping the Bands:

- Turn the loom around so the arrows are pointing toward you.
- Always use the looping tool to pick up & loop the bands.

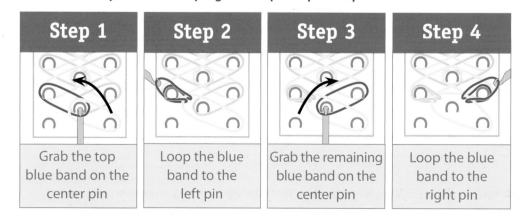

Step 1	Step 2	Step 3	Step 4
Grab the top blue band on the center pin	Loop the blue band to the left pin	Grab the remaining blue band on the center pin	Loop the blue band to the right pin

Diagram